HEAR ME, LORD

HEAR ME, LORD

Prayers from Life

MICHAEL WALKER

Fleming H. Revell Company
Old Tappan, New Jersey

First Edition 1969

© Arthur James Limited – 1969

U.S.A. and Canadian rights
Fleming H. Revell Company, N.J.

SBN: 8007-0438-x

Library of Congress Catalog Card
Number: 76-138260

MADE AND PRINTED IN GREAT BRITAIN BY PURNELL AND SONS, LTD.,
PAULTON (SOMERSET) AND LONDON

To
BERYL

FOREWORD

by

THE REV. DR. DAVID S. RUSSELL

General Secretary of the Baptist Union of Great Britain and Ireland

PRIVATE PRAYER is a frequent casualty in our distracting and all-too-busy world. To not a few Christians it is an unreal exercise, if engaged in at all, a cry for help over the gap of time and space to a God afar-off. To others it is a disciplinary exercise, however hard and unrewarding, which must be carried out for the sake of one's own soul or for the sake of the world. In such circumstances it is easy to give up private prayer altogether or else to confine oneself to the repetition of formal set prayers or simply, in the rush that is modern life, to rely entirely on ejaculatory prayer and shoot swift shafts to heaven.

The testimony of Scripture and the example of our Lord are a clear witness that prayer is much more than this. It is an experience and expression of joyous fellowship with God, a reliance upon one who knows our needs better than we know them ourselves, a recognition that our lives and the life of our world are not left in the hands of some blind Fate who weaves

7

the pattern of our destiny but of a gracious God who loves and cares and is deeply concerned about our contemporary situation.

This book by Michael Walker has been written as an expression of his own search after the reality of God in the hope that it will help others to find him also, both in their individual experience and in the very structures of the societies within which they live. My judgment is that no one can read this book without beginning to pray. It is a book of prayers which are at the same time meditations, expositions, exhortations. They are steeped in the language and thought of Scripture. But the God to whom they are addressed is no Elizabethan God; he is the Great Contemporary, the God whose concern for men overarches both time and place.

Written in modern idiom, the book is marked by a deep sincerity, an earthy reality, a penetrating insight born of personal experience and a recognition of the illimitable grace and power of God to meet the needs of men in every generation. Its text-books are the Bible and the daily newspaper. The two focuses which determine its shape and presentation are God and the world. Its concern is with God, in his infinite majesty and compassion, and with ordinary people in their helplessness apart from him. It confesses the sins of men in society and intercedes for a world exploited by greed and lust. From beginning to end it is Christ-centred, not only in its format but also in its spirit. It shows Jesus of Nazareth, who lived in a simple agricultural community, as the contemporary Christ equally at home in this highly-scientific industrial age.

I commend this book to Christians of all communions in the confidence that they will find in it not only a deepening of their own prayer life but also a new awareness of the reality of the living God.

London   DAVID S. RUSSELL

PREFACE

THERE IS NO AREA of the Christian life more susceptible to failure than that of private prayer. And because the prayer is private, the failure also is private, a burden to be carried alone with all its attendant feelings of guilt. The prayers that follow are the attempt of one man to come to terms with his own failure, for I was brought up to believe that the foundations upon which a healthy Christian life rests are public worship, the reading of the Scriptures and personal prayer. Moreover, the pattern of personal prayer was clearly defined. There was to be a certain time in the day, the Quiet Time, that one set aside for God. Order, too, was imposed upon this time by a systematic reading of scripture, a time of silent meditation and then the five-fold structured prayer of worship, confession, thanksgiving, intercession and petition.

Yet this structure that was so suited to public worship never seemed to meet the needs of private prayer. It seemed to take no account of the transition from public prayer to personal prayer. It is too obvious to be stated, but there is a whole world of difference between public and private prayer. Yet few manuals of private prayer seem to realise it, which is why many of them can equally well be used in public worship as they can in the privacy of one's own room. More so, in fact. Public prayer is addressed to the human listeners as much as to God. It needs to be clear, logical and articulate. It forms itself into statements and requests; for instance, the collects with magnificent economy all state *something*. Public utterances of any sort have to be definite and to the point if they are to hold the attention of the listener.

Too often private prayer is formed on the pattern of such public prayers, whereas in reality it resembles a conversation between two people. If one could overhear such a conversation it might seem meaningless, but it is a private and not a public utterance. Private conversations are oddly shapeless. Sometimes where there is a common understanding between the two conversationists there is no need for words; a look or a smile will suffice—words would be superfluous. Again, a sentence trails out before it is finished when the speaker realises that the listener has got the point. There is a tendency for ideas to leap about and follow no set pattern. Modern drama illustrates this well. Some people listening to a conversation in one of Harold Pinter's plays aver that people just do not speak to one another in such absurd fashion. But they do. The absurdity is only in the ear of the listener who has not yet caught the drift and real meaning of the conversation.

Private prayer is a conversation with God and more like Pinter than Cranmer! I discovered this when I tried to understand my own failure to sustain a systematic and meaningful Quiet Time. For even without those holy minutes set apart each day I was still conscious of fellowship with God, and of the whole of life being open to His influence and Spirit. I had "failed" in prayer, yet prayer was never absent from life.

When I wrote these prayers I began to explore within myself what for these past years has sufficed as prayer. It has been like dipping one's hand into a stream to catch a handful of water. I know when these prayers were written, but when they were first prayed, when they first formed themselves in my own mind and heart I know not. The stream has run by my study desk, through hospitals and the homes of the people to whom I minister, down high Scottish mountains and around the music of Bach and Brahms, in quiet places and through the tumult of a London street. Thus prayer for me has taken place in the sphere of what life *is* and not what it *ought* to be.

These prayers reflect various influences. The imagery of Scripture is never far away, for I love the Bible and its language. From *Genesis* to *Revelation* it expresses with nobility and compassion the truth about our human condition, and is lyrical in its proclamation of the sheer grace of God in coming amongst us in Jesus Christ. There is the influence of theologians; in college days John Oman, in recent years Dietrich Bonhoeffer and Pierre Teilhard de Chardin. And there is television of which I am an indiscriminate viewer, and music of which I don't hear half enough. Lastly, and most important of all, these prayers are filled with the people who have moulded my life. The woman I married. And the good people at New Southgate, Edinburgh and Highams Park amongst whom I have been honoured to bear the title of Pastor.

London   MICHAEL WALKER

ACKNOWLEDGMENTS

I WISH TO THANK the following publishers for permission to quote from their publications:
Allen and Unwin, Ltd., for a passage from Miss Pauline Webb's essay in *I Believe in God*; the Student Christian Movement Press for a quotation from Dietrich Bonhoeffer's *Letters and Papers from Prison*, and Constable and Co., Ltd., and the Rev. Dr. Harry Williams for the quotation from *The True Wilderness*.

I am also indebted to Dr. J. D. Douglas, editor of the late, and much lamented, *The Christian*, and the Rev. Walter Bottoms, editor of the *Baptist Times*. Some of these prayers first appeared in those journals, and both men have been a constant source of encouragement to me.

Finally, my thanks to Mrs. Jean Durant who by some second sight was able to read my original manuscripts and type them in the way I would have wished to type them myself; and to Philip Slaney for designing the art-work used throughout the book. Both are members of the Highams Park Baptist Church, London.

M.W.

CONTENTS

IV
VIGIL AT CALVARY

V
HE IS HERE, HE IS NOW

VI
HEAR ME, LORD

I

I Believe

The Prayers in this Section are based on
An Affirmation of Faith

1

I BELIEVE IN GOD

The Word: Mark 9 vv. 14–29

"WE DECIDE by faith that there is meaning in our lives, that there is an ultimate choice to be made freely and that the choice is directed to the love revealed to us through the Being of one perfect Man. The decision has to be made in darkness but it can be lived out in light. And even when faith fails and our hope grows dim, there remains always the possibility of love. This, for me, in the final analysis, is what it means to believe in God."[1]

Lord, I believe,
    that much I can affirm;
    I cannot, like the agnostic, argue that the
        question of Your existence is
        of no consequence: everything matters,
        and You above everything;
    I cannot opt for atheism—
        as well kick a rock and, nursing my shattered toe,
        affirm it isn't there:

Lord, I believe.

[1] Pauline Webb in *We Believe in God*, by permission.

No, Lord, my sin is not unbelief, it is wishing to be
    spared the burden of belief:
    for believing means there is
        Your will to be done,
        Your love to be lived out,
        Your Kingdom to be sought,
    and when I have done these things
    to the best of my faith, I have still known defeat like
        ashes in my mouth, and the aggression
        of people who would have accepted me with
        kindness had I not spoken Your word, and
        disillusion as I have seen the vision fossilise
            into the institution:
    Lord, I confess that at times I wish
        I didn't have to be pursued
        by faith, hope and love.
And sometimes (I confess it, Lord), I feel angry,
    angry for that man dying on a hospital bed,
        riddled with wild cells,
        plugged with obscene apparatus,
    angry for wars that will not stop,
    angry that we were made in such a way that
        virtue is always difficult,
        and iniquity so desirable:
    Lord, there are nights when, like Jacob,
        I fret for fisticuffs
        to make You tell me
        why? how? when? Who?

Lord, forgive me,
    for at every dawn You are there,
    the marks of my anger in Your hands and feet:
    I believe, and I begin to understand.

A Prayer for Others:

   for those who are indifferent,
         those who find the road to faith littered with obstacles,
      and those whose word is meant to convince, convert,
               persuade and inspire.

2

GOD IN THE CITY

The Word: Revelation 21 vv. 1–4

Dr. Ian Fraser, the Warden of Scottish Churches House, Dumblane, tells of an artisan who, finding it difficult to put his thoughts into words, each day offered his morning prayers to God in the same way. He would stand at his bedroom window, looking across the town where he lived, and hold out his hands to God. In that gesture he offered to God the life of his town for that day, and accepted the burden of his own responsibility within it.

Lord, accept this city in which I live,
    this offering I make of human achievement,
    this complex that is the work of our hands.

I would not conceal the blemishes in this offering, Lord:
    they built parts of this city with an eye to
    expediency rather than human need, hacked down the
        trees,
    covered the grass with concrete, herded too many people
    into too small a place, they made islands
    not a community;
    the woman who goes up and down to her

fifteenth-storey home in the solitude of the lift,
the people above her known only by their footsteps,
the people beneath her only when their voices
are raised in anger,
the children, driven from the stairs, who play
ball in front of the garages, dreaming of
a big stadium and the roar of
the crowd,
the girl from the small town, where everyone knew
everyone's business, curled up in her bed-sitter
with "Honey" and a paper-back
for company,
the bereaved man, alone with his sorrow, "for death
      shall no more be mentioned among you":
Lord, these I offer, and in offering make their burden mine.
And I would offer too, the wealth of this city,
      offices, industries, shops, where with eye, and mind,
      and hand people make their offering of work for the
      common good;
      schools and colleges where children and young people
      grow in understanding of the world in which they live;
      hospitals where even the poorest receive the surgeon's art,
      physician's skill, psychiatrist's insight, and the many-
      sided service of hospital staff;
      government and welfare services, child care, meals-on-
      wheels, voluntary services, youth organisations, courts,
      probation service, family service units, services for the
      physically and mentally handicapped, libraries;
      and the wealth of our culture I offer,
      music and art, concert halls, opera houses, art galleries,
      drama, comedy, theatres, cinemas, folk song, dancing.

Lord, this is our city,

I pray for the temple in the
    midst of her,
        the living body, Christ's body, the people of God,
            that they may bear the life of
                this city before You,
            and bear Christ before this city.

A Prayer for Others:
        all responsible for urban planning and the design
           of new towns,
        those who daily care for the inadequate, the
           casualties of our society,
        the church, that it may not be a ghetto.

3

THE "DEATH" OF GOD

The Word: Philippians 2 vv. 5–11

"WE CANNOT BE HONEST unless we recognize that we have to live in the world *etsi deus non daretur* (as if God were not given). And this is just what we do recognize—before God! God Himself compels us to recognize it. So our coming of age leads us to a true recognition of our situation before God. God would have us know that we must manage our lives without Him. . . . Before God and with God we live without God."[1]

Lord, is it presumption or wilful blindness to claim that "man-
        kind has come of age"?
    Bonhoeffer said we had, and the Gestapo imprisoned,
    tortured, and finally hanged him—did he believe *they* had
    attained their majority?
    we go on believing that the fist and the
    boot are more powerful persuaders than
    the word and the idea;
    chaos threatens our cities,
    and morality finds us no more mature than
    Adam and Eve, apple replete.

Lord, it is not the maturity we have found, but the innocence

[1] Dietrich Bonhoeffer in *Letters and Papers from Prison*, by permission.

we have lost, that has brought us
to mankind's adulthood:
we cannot plead ignorance,
we cannot abandon our responsibility,
for now we know:
we know the roots of insanity, the complexes,
neuroses, unconscious desires that unbalance a man,
we cannot shroud his suffering in guilt and fear;
we know what divides men of different race
and colour and we are without excuse if we
continue to nurture prejudice, unquestioned assumption,
inherited hatred;
we know the causes of calamity, we cannot wring
our hands at Aberfan, at flood or earthquake, and
piously murmur, "It is God's will";
we know the roots of war, and no war
is blessed as Your cause, or hallowed as a crusade—
all wars are *our* wars, our own wars,
our own most grievous wars:
Lord, we know; we may wish we could choose
the ignorance of our forefathers, but we cannot,
    we are burdened with responsibility,
    we have come of age.

Lord, we can no longer run from the world to find You,
    we must find You in our knowledge,
    not our ignorance,
    we must trust You in our responsibility,
    not our helplessness,
    we must seek You in every part of life,
    not in a meaningless "holy acre" that
    would fence You off from it:
Lord, in this day show us Yourself,

lest, having lost our innocence,
we do not find our maturity.

A Prayer for Others:
 for Christians who offer their priestly service to
  God in the life of industry, commerce,
  research, medicine, government;
 for the Church, that it may live within the world as
  the witness of the Resurrection.

4

EXPLORATION INTO GOD

The Word: John 14 vv. 1–7

"No, it can be no easy journey, this voyage of discovery in which
we set out to find ourselves. The road to the celestial city is a
long road. In places it must needs be stony and steep. And as we
travel we shall not always be certain of arriving at our destina-
tion. Yet from time to time we shall ascend the Delectable
Mountain, and from there we shall see the city from afar, re-
ceiving something of the breadth and length and height and
depth of what is to be fully ourselves."[1]

Lord, the memory of it is engraved in my mind,
    beating in my heart, carried in my blood,
    there, in that place, and then, at that time,
    my Damascus road, the Word was preached,
    the gates of the Kingdom swung open on
    the winds of the Spirit,
    and life became Christ.
I remember it, Lord, and sometimes the memory is a hindrance,
    it keeps me from understanding those who do not
    find this way in:
    the woman, looking for Damascus Road, waiting for

[1]H. A. Williams in *The True Wilderness*, by permission.

the blinding light from heaven that will put faith
beyond the reach of doubt,
     waiting, and I know the light will not
     come, and waiting will rob her of the
     two square feet of holy ground she
     already has, enough to take her stand;
the teenager, conditioned to live life without You,
to whom You are at best an optional extra—
     He is the most difficult of all;
     I cannot imagine any reality without You,
     yet I must if I am to
     understand him;
the man, prejudice formed, habits hardened,
for whom there is nothing new under the sun
(and some seed fell on stony ground).
     Is there a way into him that can
     become his way into You?

Lord, it seems they have closed their hearts to You, help me
     not to close my heart to them, in mistaken zeal,
     as if your heart were closed to them:
     the cross, Lord, it is open to all,
     its arms can be extended into infinity,
     it does not exclude, it embraces;
     they forget You, You forget none, every
     man is remembered by You:
may I be open to others, Lord,
     to this woman, haunted by past failures,
     who did her best but it was
     never quite good enough, no longer prepared
     to run the risk of failure;
     to this teenager, angry for Vietnam, emotional,
     to whom the prize of love is clearly seen

yet always elusive;
this man, whose dreams died, remembering
in life's afternoon the ecstasy of the morning,
seeing with anxiety the first signs
of evening's approach.
Lord, help me to walk with them,
    to resist the temptation of short-cutting to what was
        my time and my place, my Damascus Road,
    believing Your love knows no weariness, and that there is
        no end to your patience.

A Prayer for Others:
    those for whom present faith is made difficult by past
        failures,
    those who look for God at the perimeter of life instead
        of in the things that concern them most deeply,
    for the testimony of Christians.

II

His Coming amongst Us

The Prayers in this Section are based on
The Birth of Christ

1

THE STAR

The Word: Matthew 2 vv. 1–18

LORD, there is not enough light in myself to guide me:
    reason throws its light on the path in
    front of me, but sometimes the darkness is
    stronger than reason;
        the world is not always reasonable, but dark,
        irrational, absurd, cruel,
        (I do not know *why* men suffer, *why* evil
        feasts on our human fears and hatreds, *why* good
        men perish because they are good:
        reason cannot tell me *why*);
    when reason's light fails, my heart can
    take me on a few more steps:
        I feel truth I cannot understand,
        I apprehend with my flesh and blood mysteries
            that my mind cannot explain:
        yet my heart can be traitor,
            fickle in its love,
            opening its doors to darkness
                as much as light.

Lord, there is not enough light in myself to guide me.

You have set a star in my heavens that I might
follow it, Lord:
  a star whose light pierces up and down and out
  like the beams of a cross,
  a star risen never again to plunge into the earth
  like a dead man:
  I see its light, Lord,
    in the word of a preacher,
    in the faith of a friend,
    in the eyes of those I love,
    in a hand stretched up to
      grasp my compassion,
    in the courage of those who
      resist adversity,
    in the darkness that men have
      made and I have made.
  I see its light, Lord,
    and I know that I must follow it.

It isn't easy, Lord, it couldn't have been easy for them:
  wise men on a fool's errand,
  leaving the security and prestige of home,
  padding across the deserts,
  tangled in political duplicity,
  looking for a king without a crown,
    without a kingdom,
  without power, without name;
  yet they followed, Lord, risking everything.

That star in my heavens beckons me, Lord: give me faith,
  give me faith, Lord, lest I choose the
  worldly wisdom of the uncommitted, and caution
  root my feet in the ground while

that star pursues its journey to be lost forever from
my sight;
give me faith, Lord, lest fear keep
me from that journey; (there is
wilderness, Lord, and I don't like thirst
and solitude; there are steep paths,
aching limbs, bursting lungs; there are
heights, risk, exposure, there is a
valley, and rod and staff seem
so inadequate);
give me faith, Lord, lest I say
the light of that star is not enough,
and I wait for a larger light,
for a sun instead of a star,
and waiting for that dawn
I perish in this night;
give me faith, Lord, to follow the
light I see and trust that it is
always enough for the next step.

So bring me to that place where every light gathers,
    where He is, whose kingdom is earth,
        whose kingly robes are
           this flesh and blood,
        whose cause is justice,
        whose way is peace,
        whose power is love,
        whose name is "God-with-us":
    and I know that the journey
        was as nothing:
    the place where this star comes to rest,
        everything.

A Prayer for Others:

   for the cautious, who wait
   for the reckless, who do not count
      the cost,
   for those who see no star.

2

THE SHEPHERDS

The Word: Luke 2 vv. 8–20

THE NIGHT-SHIFT is always the longest, the hours pass
    reluctantly from ten to six;
    it is a time for talk, for at night everything
    is clear;
    the grey problems that beset us focus sharply into
    black and white, the tongue discovers an eloquence that
    would sound absurd by day;
    it is a time for small talk,
        where does the money go?
        how that goal was set up or lost,
        what the President said,
        my son learned to ride his bike today,
        the court case reported in the papers, funny business,
        the Wednesday Movie—glad to get out and come to
            work!
    the words chase each other,
    the eyes grow heavy,
    men sitting, their faces illuminated by their cigarettes like
    carnival masks in a pleasure garden,

Sometimes they stumble on religion,
    it's all been disproved, of course,

37

the vicar and his crumbling old steeple,
the new-fangled hymns (listening one would think
        there was a time when every service
        began with "Abide With Me" and
        ended with "The Day Thou Gavest")
the hypocrites—
    this is religion
      not who can forgive me?
      who can wash my guilt away?
      who can call love out of me?
      how heal the wounds of hatred, mistrust,
        aggression?
      whose hands shall hold me when I die?

That is how it was, outside Bethlehem, in the fields, on the
        pastoral night-shift,
        men's faces lit by the smoking fire,
        talking of home, wife, children,
        the price of sheep,
        the wolf they chased over the hill today,
        politics, the damned Romans;
   and religion,
        at least you don't have Pharisees snooping round
          these fields,
        seeing that you keep the law,
        and the priests are too busy with their city politics,
        and the synagogue is just as it always was,
          scripture, psalms,
          preachers dry as dust.

"There were shepherds abiding in the fields. . . ."
    Lord, how we have surrounded them with our piety and
        crowned them with the hoary holiness of the
        centuries;

made them theologians of perception, listening to
Gabriel with doctrinally attuned ears:
men of sensibility and musical appreciation, hearing
in the angelic choir the fugal structures of Bach
and the sweeping chords of Beethoven;
surely, the heavenly battalions would be wasted
on lesser men.
And so we sunder them from their successors who still
sit and talk through the night-shift
and nothing we say will make *them* tumble
down the hillside to Bethlehem;
they do not hear our Gospel as Good News.

Lord, it was Good News on the hillside that night,
Christ born in their trivial world,
to take the curse of sin from men's hearts,
Christ born, made man, wrapped in woollen cloth,
rocked in cradle-trough,
Glory, glory, glory, God's favour rests on men—
the likes of us men!
Lord, give us Gabriel's tongue,
that we may tell men of Christ,
the night-shift men,
who do not recognize good music,
but rejoice at Good News.

A Prayer for Others:
working-class people to whom the
church is alien territory,
the church, ministering in industrial
towns and cities,
for Christians who work on the
factory floor.

3

THE STABLE

The Word: Luke 2 vv. 1–7

LORD, my Christmas cards are covered in stables:
　　each one a focus of devotion, a place of light,
　　that greets me like a fire in winter;
　　the straw looks dry and sweet-smelling,
　　the animals as friendly as the toys in my
　　　　children's bedroom,
　　and Mary, pink and beautiful, like any new mother
　　in the maternity ward,
　　with Joseph looking on, a wise, unruffled old man.

Lord, how far from Bethlehem are the stables on my Christmas
　　cards?
　　how far from that night, when Joseph carried his
　　　　young wife,
　　her body jerking in the spasms of labour,
　　and laid her on the stable floor
　　　　—(is there comfort in straw laid on a
　　　　　stone floor?)
　　whilst donkeys disturbed, blinked and grunted their
　　　　protest.

That night, when Jesus was born,
   was *born*:
   Joseph, lover, husband, and mid-wife,
      clutching the hand that sought for his in that
      elated moment as the child's head made its last
      thrust from the matrix;
      receiving the baby, slippery wet and blood streaked,
      screwed up face, tiny clenched hands,
      a cry,
      cutting the navel cord, sundering him
      from his mother and giving him to the world,
      (was there water in the stable to wash clean
      the new baby?)
      wrapping him in the bands the thoughtful girl
      had carried from Nazareth,
      giving the child to her, her hair sticking to
      the sweat on her face, grey with exhaustion
      —that night, when Jesus was born,
         was *born*.

Lord, how far is it to Bethlehem?
   —where is that stable now?
   it is in this city, Lord,
      where a mother gives birth to her boy
      in the one room that is their home,
      the dismal wall-paper (they put it up in
      the 20's when the middle-class folk lived here)
      hangs tattered from the wall, they carry boiling water
      from the gas ring on the landing, brothers and
      sisters stir in their sleep at the baby's cry,
      whilst father drowns his inadequacy at the inn where
      there is always room, until it is time to
      greet his new-born with a beery kiss;

it is in places of hunger, Lord,
>
> where a mother's breasts hang milkless, and if
> a child survives they will stuff him with starch
> that will fatten his belly and strip his ribs,
> and one day he may cry like Job that
> it were better they had carried him from the
> womb to the grave on the day
> of his birth;

it is in the place of war, Lord,
>
> where a child is born to violence, and
> tomorrow his mother may clutch him as they
> run to another place of safety, always running
> from bullets, bombs, flame, the tramp of boots,
> the grinding of tanks, the shriek of aircraft.

How far is it to Bethlehem?
>
> Lord, that Christmas card will hide the
> truth from us if I let it,
>> it will hide the night that Jesus was
>> born, was *born*,
>> it will hide the stables where, even now,
>> a child is born.

A Prayer for Others:
>
> *remember the work of the Red Cross and other*
> *rescue projects in our society,*
> *and the work of the Salvation Army and the*
> *missionary societies overseas,*
> *and men of compassion who choose to live*
> *in, and share, the poverty of others.*

4

THE CHILD

The Word: John 1 vv. 1–14

LORD, You put Your life into our hands,
there is nothing more defenceless than a baby,
and Your life was at risk.

You risked the inhumanity of bureaucrats, with their fussy
minds, tabulating, listing, issuing orders with no
thought of the people expected to comply with them,
always insisting that the rules be kept, because to
think or to feel would be chaos:
the rules must be kept, and a pregnant girl, her nine
months nearly up, must risk a hundred miles on
a donkey's back, jolting, swaying, back-breaking, to
become in Bethlehem a tick on someone's list;
You risked the indifference of people who never want
to know—you can't turn away a girl in labour
and her husband pale with fear for her;
but the stable is at the back, out of sight,
and above the sound of talking, shouting, laughter,
coins, a baby's cry will not be heard, or better,
a silence go unnoticed;
You risked the cruelty of power, the power of

43

the insecure, the jealous, the obsessed; power that
would smash out the brains of every first-born
boy, power that would serve up a prophet's head
on a plate for the price of a skirt.

You put Yourself at risk to our inhumanity, Lord, and You
trusted Yourself to our humanity:
You trusted Mary not to betray the sacred responsibility
of life borne within her womb, but to carry,
to bring forth, and to nurture;
You trusted Joseph not to be a faithless man, but
to carry the woman who bore the child,
to comfort and say a thousand times he
loved her, to fend for her and
find her a place to deliver the child,
Mary's child, his child, whose father he
knew not . . .
You trusted the integrity of wise men, that
they would not betray what they had discovered,
nor disclose what they had seen, but chose
to worship in a stable rather than conspire
with kings.

Lord, so was the Word made flesh,
threatened by our inhumanity,
embraced by our humanity, like flesh embracing bone.
Lord, forgive that cruelty that still puts the Word
at risk,
forgive us when we try to
mould men to fit systems, instead of making
systems to fit men,
forgive us if we allow the state to
crush the weak instead of protecting them,

44

forgive us when we push from our sight
what is unpleasant, the terrible dilemmas of others,
the tragic;
forgive us when we will not act until first
we have moralised and lectured,
forgive us if we do not protest at the
abuse of power.
And, Lord, confirm our humanity,
that we may accept the sacred responsibility of
bearing this human flesh that You bore,
that we may love with tenderness,
that we may protect the weak, though it
provoke the threat of the strong

—that this all too earthy flesh
may bear something of that
glory
that was seen in Him,
Jesus, full of grace and truth.

A Prayer for Others:

*those who have to preserve their humanity
in the face of brutality, cruelty and power,
for all who hold power, and abuse it.*

III

The Man
for Others

The Prayers in this Section are based on
The Ministry of Christ

1

A FRIEND FOR ALL

The Word: Mark 2 vv. 13–17

LORD, how easily it rolls off the tongue,
    "Publicans and sinners,"
    they have become part of the Biblical hierarchy,
    angels, archangels, prophets, apostles, publicans and
        sinners,
    their presence no longer shocks us.
    Your friendship for them has ceased to amaze us,
    we applaud Your concern for them,
    as long as they can remain *Your* publicans and sinners.

What were they like, Lord?
    did some of them have greedy hands, never missing
    an opportunity for a dishonest penny?
    did the tax-collectors have their private in-jokes,
    laughing like drains at things others found
    unamusing?
    did they nudge one another and exchange knowing looks
    when they saw Mary of Magdalene?
    were they uncommitted to anything save their own
        interests?

Lord, we read about them in church,
would it embarrass us if they were actually there?

We haven't any "publicans and sinners" around here, Lord, at
    least, we don't call them that;
    lay-abouts, malingerers, neurotics, immoral persons,
    grabbing, shifty—that's what we call them, and we
    can't always see that we should love them,
    our publicans and sinners.

Mary lives in one room,
    she has had two children, one is in care and
    one living with her,
    she had an abortion at the third pregnancy;
    she has no husband,
    and the men wait outside her door to have some
    sex from her for a dollar a time,
    a dollar, Lord!—who was redeemed at the price
    of Calvary.

And there's the lass in the new council flat,
    with her daughter,
    and the man who isn't her husband,
    who ducks every responsibility he has to her and
    the child,
    turns up when he feels like it,
    gives her house-keeping money when he has it or
    remembers it,
    over whom she has no legal claim whatever
        —as you know, Lord, this is a
        swinging, permissive society.

Lord, people like these were Your friends,

we have to be taught a friendship
like that:
give us something of Your love, Lord,
because ours would break into a thousand
pieces at the first rebuff
  —and if love means anything we have to
  face numerous rebuffs, and endless disappointments.

They are *our* publicans and sinners, Lord,
  You have accepted them,
  help us to do the same.

A Prayer for Others:
  Remember the most unlikely people
   and pray for them.

2

JESUS THE TEACHER

The Word: Matthew 5 vv. 1–12

LORD, words are in danger,
    we hear thousands of them,
    they are used to beat us into believing things we don't
        want to believe,
    they are manipulated as propaganda,
    they are ornamented to hide the falsehood in the half-truth,
    they are rent by double-talk,
    they are bloated with exaggeration,
    they are weapons of war;
    given different meanings, they sow dissension and
        confusion:
    words, words, words,
    we are losing our faith in them, Lord.
    I want words to mean what they say, Lord,
    so I come to You,
    Word made flesh,
    and believing the integrity of that incarnation
        I believe the words You spoke.

We have tried to prostitute Your words, Lord, but they remain
    chaste;

we imagine we have exhausted their meaning,
and then they come to us with new significance like
    a resurrection;
they are simple, yet touch the depths of human life,
they are few, yet sufficient for us to know
    what is truth.
They reverse our values, Lord,
    for we admire those who can make money,
    and push grief from our sight;
    the gentle get trodden down,
    and there's enough injustice to make us lose
        our appetite for righteousness;
    mercy is soft,
    and purity old-fashioned;
    the peace-makers have no chance against the aggressors,
    and there are no causes worth suffering for, let alone
        dying for.
These are our falsehoods
    smothered in our words.

Yet with my own eyes I have seen the truth,
    in poverty, tears, gentleness, crusading passion,
        forgiveness, chastity, reconciliation, faithfulness,
I have seen values that cannot be destroyed:
I have seen the blessed:
earth would perish tomorrow were they not among us.

A Prayer for Others:

    Pray through the Beatitudes
        —at each one think of a particular person
        whose life is characterised by that quality
        —pray for them.

3

JESUS THE HEALER

The Word: Mark 1 vv. 32–34; 2 vv. 1–12

LORD, it must have seemed like the dawn of the Kingdom,
   God's reign established over the enemies of man,
   pain, disease, death,
   as You healed the sick and booted out the devils.
   With astonished gratitude they saw the coming of
   the Kingdom:

   a dumb man, tongue liberated, throat full of voice,
   shouting a psalm of David to the four winds;
   a lame man, throwing away his crutch like a caber,
   dancing before the ark of God:
   a blind man, stooping to wash the mud from his eyes,
   and seeing his reflection in Siloam's waters;
   a woman, her secret shame taken from her;
   a father, rocking his child in the sleep of innocence,
   remembering the madness that had tortured the boy's
   body and foamed at his mouth
       —these saw the Kingdom come.

Lord, men are still being made whole;
   since You came amongst us, we refuse to stand

defeated before disease:
the miracles go on,
in operating theatre, in the use of drugs,
in psycho-analysis,
illness is being defeated, men live who should
have died, sleep peacefully who would have been
in pain,
because You came amongst us as One Who heals.

Lord, for my friends who have been healed, thank You;
yet I remember too, those who knew salvation in Christ,
who had to wait for the redemption of their bodies:
Stan, paralysed, his arms and hands bent by the disease
that waged war on his spine, his strong spirit nurtured on
Christ, the scriptures and his hymn-book (does
he discuss with the angels what tune they should use for
"Worthy the Lamb", Lord?);
Em, artistic brilliance run to schizophrenic confusion;
Vera, whose body disease plundered mercilessly before it
handed her over to kind death in her thirty-fourth year.

Lord, we look with such as these for the coming of Your
Kingdom,
we pit our prayers against the powers of corruption,
and, by the risen body of Jesus, we look with hope to
what is yet to come.

A Prayer for Others:

Pray for someone who is ill,
first by trying to understand all
that the illness means to him,
then offering your understanding to God.

4

TEMPTATION

The Word: Luke 4 vv. 1–13

LORD, we expect more of others than we do of ourselves,
their temptations differ from ours,
what tempts them would never tempt us,
what to them is so desirable is to us steeped in
the ordinary and common-place,
what to them holds the sweetness of forbidden fruit
is to us no more tempting than a crab-apple;
we do not have to be thrown about by the violence
of the desires that tempt others:
so we are without sympathy,
and worse, blind to the sins that assail us.

Lord, we do not know what it is to be deprived,
deprived of love and security within a family,
of encouragement at school, of creative satisfaction
at work: we do not know the deprivation that clenches
into anger, and the anger that erupts into violence;
we do not always understand what makes other people love
each other,
those two fail to attract us, we cannot see what
they see in each other, and not sharing their passion,

we cannot know their temptations:
we do not have that terrible discontent that looks to the
    Bingo jack-pot, or the racetrack finally to
    resolve life's problems;

Lord, we are not tempted like these,
    which tempts us to believe that we have no temptations.

Ours come clothed as virtue, Lord,
    like a Devil mouthing texts;
    our enthusiasm for the Kingdom becomes enthusiasm for
    our "kingdoms", for we like the heady heights of power:
    the power of "the word" that is not always Christ's word,
    but our word, angry and violent, expecting submission,
    powerful as a sword,
    the power to exercise authority in our little "kingdom",
    to be "someone" among the people of God, carrying the
    symbols of our authority like sceptres: minute books,
    vestments, the honours of office, the teapot at the
    women's meeting,
    the power of service, the temptation to
    place others in our debt by what we do for
    them out of interested love.

Lord, You drove the devil back,
    because only by the sacrifice of the cross
    could come resurrection
    and our redemption.
    Help us to understand ourselves,
        to see clearly the enormity of the spiritual
            sins that tempt us,
        and so learn compassion for those
            who fight (what are to us)
            their lesser battles.

A Prayer for Others:

> *Let us pray for those who have*
> *no purpose, no morality,*
> *no commitment, no obligation,*
> *that enable them to resist temptation.*

5

SACRIFICE

The Word: Matthew 16 vv. 13–28

LORD, we are not strangers to the language of sacrifice,
    the history of the church is soaked in it;
        men, women and youths have suffered every torment,
        pain, indignity, cruelty and deprivation that the mind
        of man can invent, rather than betray the faith,
        and, for good measure, Christians have hounded
            Christians,
        and we have all been given our martyrs at one another's
        hands, the Protestants their Latimer, the Catholics
            their Thomas More,
        and Thomas Helwys, of blessed Baptist
            memory;

    the worship of the church is redolent with it, our hymns
        urge us to the upward way, harsh and flinty,
        we are exhorted to bear the cross, our baptism
        is a death and burial, while constantly the communion
        speaks to us of a sacrifice made once and
        for all
            —Lord, the language of sacrifice we know well,
            it is the experience we seem to lack.

We worship openly and none forbids us,
  we preach the word as we believe it, and nobody
  hastens to report us to the police,
  we are free to teach our children the truths of
  the Christian faith, we are not brought to trial,
  imprisoned, refused work, ostracized, humiliated.
Lord, we thank You that You gave others the faith
    to make their sacrifice,
    in order that we need not make it.

Yet, Lord, there is a chafing of the shoulder,
  and a weight upon the spirit,
  even for us, the cross is inescapable:

  You have called us to believe in a time of doubt,
  in which every authority is questioned, every
  conviction received with scepticism, every
  article of faith subject to incredulity;

  You have called us to the way of Christ, passionate and
  compassionate, committed, idealist, revolutionary, at a
  time when every crusade is wedded to violence;

  You have called us to be peace-makers, to feel
  in the reconciling body of Christ the pain of those
  who are divided and torn by hatred and mistrust;

Lord, help us to discern the cross we bear,
  our sacrifice is not dying for the faith, it is
  living for it.

A Prayer for Others:
  Let us remember all who suffer, in other parts of the
      world, for their faith,
  let us remember the work of Legal Aid,
      and all who are imprisoned illegally.

6
THE CROSS

The Word: Galatians 6 vv. 14–18

LORD, help me sometimes to stand on the other side of the
  empty tomb, that, understanding Calvary more deeply,
  I may live in the Resurrection more fully:

  there was defeat, Lord, not apparent, short-lived
  defeat, but defeat that must have seemed final, permanent
  and irreversible: the gentle do not inherit the earth
  after all, they are crushed by the powerful;

  there was loneliness, Lord; it should not have been,
  there were eleven who could have watched, but to pain
  was added the loss of friends whose loyalty had been
  promised on oaths stronger than death;

  there was pain, and no telling how long it would
  last; and there was death, to be endured in the faith
  that a resurrection would come; it was to come,
  but first the seed must fall into the ground
  (He was crucified ... dead ... buried).

Lord, help me to stand on the other side of the
  empty tomb,

for that is where some people have to stand:
those whose cause is defeated, for whom justice
comes too late to right the unequal balance,
those who see violence have its way,
and love kicked aside,
those for whom pain is not a refining fire,
a character-building, ennobling experience, but a
torment bringing fear, loss and bitterness,
those for whom death is not a consummation, but a
tragic interruption, an untimely end, a bearer of grief;

Lord, these know in their bones a Calvary
I can only know in my imagination and
in fellowship with them.

Lord, help me to stand on the other side of the
empty tomb,
for You stand there now—visiting the souls who
are in prison (He descended into hell);
their cause is Yours,
their darkness You have shared,
their suffering You bear (behold My hands . . .),
their death You have died,
    and in You, at the last, they shall
      live.

Lord, help me to stand on the other side of the
empty tomb . . . sometimes.

A Prayer for Others:
    those who find it hard to believe that love
      is stronger than hate,
    those who must come to a resurrection like Christ's,
    through suffering like Christ's.

62

IV

Vigil at Calvary

The Prayers in this Section are based on
The Seven Words from The Cross

1

FORGIVENESS

The Word: Luke 23 v. 34

And Jesus said, Father, forgive them, for they know not what they do.

LORD, to Your disciples, that day at Calvary must have seemed
all darkness and defeat: did it seem like that to You?
Your hands, carpenter's hands, hands that touched the
leper and blessed the child, were twisted and splintered
as they drove in the nails.
Your body, the temple of God, they stripped and stretched
out like a bow.

Did you long to protest Your innocence? To cry out
for justice?
Did you want to tell the men who crucified You
that one day they would kneel before You, when
the sons of God would rise to the new day
like the great rays of the sun, and all creation
kneel in the gratitude of the redeemed?

Lord, it was neither Your innocence that concerned You, nor
the Resurrection to come that lightened that darkness:
their guilt was Your concern,
it was forgiveness not hope that transfigured that
moment.

c   65

Father, forgive them . . .

> Lord, there are people today who suffer in the darkness;
> who, though innocent, receive violence and cruelty at
> the hands of their fellow men.
>
> We pray that the darkness of inhumanity may still be
> transfigured by the forgiveness that stems from the cross.
> Father, forgive them:
>
>> the hirelings of all totalitarian systems who seek to
>> enslave men's minds;
>>
>> all who use power to coerce, to cripple and to
>> humiliate those who are weak;
>>
>> those who prey upon the fears of others and
>> exploit their guilt;
>>
>> the cruel ones: the thug, the gossip-monger, the
>> aggressively insecure, the thoughtless.
>
> Forgive them, and be the source of all hope,
> and light and strength,
> to those who suffer at their hands.

For they know not what they do . . .

> That's the terrible thing, Lord, so much evil done with
> so little thought; men who do what they believe is
> their duty, or what is required of them, or what is
> expedient, and in so doing bring guilt upon themselves.
> And Lord, so it is with us. It is easy in church
> to confess to You that we are "miserable offenders" and yet
> not realise the misery of our offence. It is easier to
> recognise the damage done by the sins of others, than to
> acknowledge our sins for what they are.
>
> When we are vehement and angry in our opinions it is
> because we are afraid that we shall be proved wrong,
> that our pride will fall like Lucifer from heaven;

our concern is with ourselves and not with truth.
We use words as if they had no meaning for others,
we forget the violence of what we say; we chatter
interminably when we should be silent, and are silent
when our voices should ring from house-tops.
We confess our faith in Your forgiveness and yet harbour
resentments month after impious month; we take umbrage,
we have a keen sense of our rights.
We say with our lips "Jesus Christ is risen! Hallelujah!"
and we live as if He were dead.

Father, forgive us, for we know not what we do . . .
My son, go in peace, your sins have been forgiven.

A Prayer for Others:
   for those who have been wronged, and who
      cannot forgive,
   for those who have wronged others, and
      see no need of forgiveness,
   for those who confess sins they do not commit,
      and are blind to those they do.

2

REDEMPTION

The Word: Luke 23 v. 43

Jesus said, Truly I say to you, today you will be with me in Paradise.

LORD, Your disciples had staked their claim to the places at
    Your right and left hands in the Kingdom:
    but when the throne of the cross was lifted up,
        when the thorned crown was crushed upon Your head,
        when Your hands were outstretched, bearing the orb
            and sceptre of nails,
    it was criminals, not disciples, they lifted on the crossed
    thrones at Your right and left hand.

Who were they, Lord, and what their crime?
    Had they murdered, fiercely in zeolot passion for freedom,
        or brutally for gain, a human life for a
        handful of coins?
    Treachery, violence, greed, lust, revenge—what had
        brought
        them to this death?
    What marks had the vicious years etched on their
        features—
        cruel mouth; depthless, shifting eyes; hard, furrowed
        flesh?

68

Two men, Lord, attendants at a world's redemption, unwilling
    acolytes
        at the sacrifice of the Anointed, once, and for all.
Two men, Lord,
    and one cursed the justice that punished his guilt, reviled
    an innocence he no longer understood, despised the
        weakness
    that bore with a cross;
    and one, that day, went to Paradise.

Lord Jesus, how did it happen? How did this man recognize
    the King?
    how glimpse Paradise at the place of the skull?
    He saw a Man, Lord, with body broken like his own;
    He witnessed his own dying, for Your death, Lord,
        was as his death;
    He saw One Who had no form nor comeliness that
        any should desire Him:
    Despised, as he was despised, rejected, as he was rejected,
        a Man of sorrows, acquainted with his grief.

Is that how it happened, Lord Jesus?
    The innocent broken, as with his guilt,
    One dying and one death, that was his dying
        and his death,
    goodness, made of no reputation, as he was
        of no repute.
    A Man who bore all his sorrow,
        and infinitely more.
The Son of God, Who loved me and gave Himself for me.

So, Lord Jesus Christ, You have given us Paradise, for we
    are as dying malefactors.

We forget so quickly that the Kingdom of Heaven was
      opened to us at the cross; we look within
      ourselves for motive for Your love—our righteousness,
      our moral rectitude, our purity, our impeccable
      respectability;
      even *our* faith, and *our* good acts, as if
      faith had given birth to Calvary, and goodness were
      the measure of *our* love.
Lord, remind us, with memories that are purging fire, until we
    forget no more.
    The cross of that dying thief is our cross, our
      guilt, our desert, our death:
    and You, Lord, bore that same cross, and upon
      You was laid the iniquity of us all.

Lord, remember us when You come in Your Kingdom.
    The cross we have earned, but You have given us
      Paradise.

A Prayer for Others:
    for those who have to face their worst crises
      alone,
    for men who know their guilt, that they may
      know their Saviour.

3

LOVE

The Word: John 19 vv. 26–27

Jesus said, Mother, behold thy son; Behold thy mother.

LORD, back there in the Garden, in the moment when loyalty and courage were put to the test, Your disciples ran away; the arrest, the trials, the burdensome march to this place, You bore alone, without the comfort of friend, without the support of even one who would vouch for the truth of Your words and testify to what he had received at Your hands.

And now, in this place of cruelty and hostility, these two dare to stand, knowing that words will not console, nor pity take away pain, nor love bring You down from the cross: Mary and John.

Mary who bore You, into whose heart the sword has now
    pierced;
Mary who gave birth to and nurtured this body that men
    have now broken;
Mary, full of memories—Gabriel, Bethlehem, Nazareth, kind
    and faithful Joseph, the laughter of children playing in
    the street, the sweet, clean smell of planed wood, the son

she loved whose ways were beyond her understanding.

John, whom You called from his fishing—was it only three
      years ago?
John, as passionate in his hatred as in his love;
John, who understood so much more than the others, yet
        even so,
      understood so little of the whole truth.

Lord Jesus, the love with which they watch in silence is an
      offering that others would make were they here:
      they see You, with eyes full of grief, as Bartimaeus
      would see You were he here now;
      if there were words of sympathy to offer they would
      speak them as would stricken men whose tongues you
      set free;
      they stand sentinel at this cross, as men whose crooked
      limbs You straightened would stand were they here;
      they stand—representative of every man, woman and
        child
      to whom Your hands were healing, Your presence
      blessing,
      Your words eternal life.
And what they offer, Lord, Your words now make holy—
      Mother, son;
      Son, mother;
      You have sanctified the bonds of human love, friendship,
      affection, kindness;
      You have hallowed the frail and vulnerable web of human
      relationships within which our lives are set.

Lord, we accept them every day, the gifts of love that others
      offer us, accept them as if they were ours by right,

take them with greedy hands with no thought of their cost,
taking for granted kindness, consideration, understanding,
loyalty, affection and service.
Lord, sometimes we are so obsessed with our own needs that
we fail to see the needs of others;
sometimes we use people for our own ends, shoulders
on which to weep, friends of convenience, statistics of
our success, useful contacts;
sometimes we fail in our natural duties to wife, husband,
brother, sister, mother, father, children, lover, friend;
we stretch their loyalty, strive to mould them in our own
image, accept what they do for us in our times of stress
and forget them in theirs.

Lord, touch again all our human loving with Your love, for in
the midst of Your agony, You forgot neither family nor
friend.

A Prayer for Others:
   *remember families under stress, through illness,
      separation or bereavement,
   and families where love has gone cold.*

4

DESOLATION

The Word: Matthew 27 vv. 45–46

Jesus cried with a loud voice, My God, my God, why hast thou forsaken me?

LORD, there was another hillside, where once You spoke of God's
care for all that He had made:
You stooped and picked a wild flower—the pageantry of
Solomon's court was tawdry compared to the care and
artistry God had lavished on this, You said;
as birds wheeled in flight above the crowds, shrill
song, swift descent, God feeds them, You said;
and You looked at the men, women and children around
You—the hairs on your head are counted, God knows you
all, You said.

Lord, this is not that hillside, no pilgrims Temple-bound
come here,
no children know this place, only ghouls who can watch
another man's pain;
no flowers grow amidst these rocks, the fallen seed
is snatched away, or dies in the sun;
birds of song are banished, this is the territory of
vultures;

here the hairs on a man's head, his limbs, his flesh,
 his mind, his senses are as nothing, human life
 is cheap.
Where is now your God?

Lord Jesus, that cry from the cross makes us tremble: and fills
 us with hope.
  We know that place where God is, His Presence
   felt, His Spirit known;
  we know too that place where it seems that God
   is not, the Abyss into which we plunge
   either by our own treachery or the
   cruel circumstance that throws us down
   into darkness;
  the Abyss, Lord, Lord Jesus, Holy Son of God the
   Father, You know it too, deeper than
   any depths we can imagine, a darkness beyond our
   conceiving, the darkness of God's absence into which
   He enters for Whom God is All
   and in All.
  And now, Lord, everywhere, even where it seems
   that God is not, You are there.
If I make my bed in hell, You are there also.

How often in this generation, Lord, has Your cry been wrung
 from men's lips. We remember them, those who felt
 forsaken by God:
   the Jewish child, naked, shorn head, torn from
   parents, choking gas in the terrible death of
   Auschwitz;
   the family, father, mother, children, huddled in
   their home as bullets rake the street of their
   Vietnamese village:

a man who watches cancer invade the body of a
loved one, and sees pain that knows no
pity destroy without haste;
the black man bearing insult, "Nigger!" from
loose lips, "Blacks need not apply" from
advertisement column.

Lord, their cry is Your cry:
    You have been where they are,
    there is no going beyond Your Presence.

We pray that You will give to them the grace of Calvary:
    the grace which, having endured the moment
    when God is no more, finds that God is All.

A Prayer for Others:
    those who pass through dark experiences, and
        feel that their prayers are unanswered,
    those for whom faith is sometimes against all
        the visible evidence,
    those who feel abandoned.

5

GIVING

The Word: John 19 v. 28

Jesus said, I thirst.

LORD, they offered You drink before ever they stretched You
out on the cross:
the good women of Jerusalem, driven by some Israelite
compassion to this hillside where no woman should be;
women who, death march after death march, offered what
little there was to offer to those whose sealing doom
was so near;
a compound offered to executed criminals, to numb sense,
to drive the mind to the borders of delirium where dreams
and phantasies might be kinder than reality, a drug to
wage unequal battle against piercing nail, twisted muscle
and taut nerve;

You refused that drink, Lord, the drug that strove to turn
the pangs of the cross into the twilight world
of Sheol.
As man You had lived, Word incarnate, flesh, blood, senses,
nerves, tissues, effort, rest, childhood, youth, manhood;
as man You would die, accepting for us men the
burdens of eternity that we carry in this all too

77

vulnerable body. For you, no retreat, no drugged journey
out of Calvary, but the bearing of our whole human condition.

Now, Lord, the limping hours are reaching their end; Your
leathered tongue, cracked lips, throat of dust,
cry for relief:
Jesus, Son of God, You thirst.

You thirst Who, in the beginning, separated the sea
and the dry land, Who sent sparkling streams running
down hill and mountain, Who formed the rivers that
moved with majesty through the land to be lost
in the great seas;
You thirst Who, in Israel's wilderness and thirst, gave
water gushing from the rock;
You thirst Who offered to all who thirsted wine and milk,
without money and without price.
You thirst Who offered a Samaritan woman living water
that would never fail.

Lord, out of the wealth You had given, they offer back
a sponge, soaked in vinegar, raised on a spear,
to slake Your parched lips with bitterness.
It was the last thing we gave to You in
Your earthly ministry, our last vain attempt to quench with
gall the eternal flaming love glimpsed here at
this cross.

Your voice is still heard, Lord, did You not promise
that it would be so?
Hands reach up for a cup of cold water,
and Your voice is heard in famine, in cities diseased
by the disruption of war, in places where the
cisterns have been poisoned by conflict and neglect,

where earthquakes and natural disasters have polluted
water so that no man can drink it and still live:
Lord, the voices are claimant and their voice is Yours—I thirst.

And again, Lord it is ours to give or to withhold.

A cup of cold water given in Your Name is
    given to You; You have filled earth with
    the gifts we have to give to those
    in need.
But, Lord, You know us. The real meaning of that
    cry may be lost on us, we may reach
    for the nearest sop to hand, we may act as
    if to salve our consciences more than to
    slake Your thirst, we may still offer gall from
    the distance of benevolence, instead of holding
    with our own hands the cup of water
    to the lips of a needy man.
Lord, You know us. Do not let us escape. May
    the voice of millions be the voice of the
    Christ, I thirst.
    Lord, You have placed in our hands a cup
    of cold water—water, Lord, not vinegar.
Lord Jesus, if only I could have been there and
    given it to You then.
Lord Jesus, in my neighbour You are here; may I
    give it to You now.

A Prayer for Others:
    those for whom a cup of water is a
        priceless treasure,
    those who are dependent on other men's
        compassion, and other men's action,
        if they are to survive.

79

6

DARKNESS

The Word: John 20 v. 30

Jesus said, It is finished.

LORD, the chattering and abuse of the crowd ended some hours
ago;
   after that there were few sounds in that crushed silence,
      the rattle of dice, the spoils already gambled away,
      the monotony of men who wait for a six to fall and
      three men to die;
      the weeping of those for whom tears would soon be
      overtaken by grief unable to cry any more;
      the quiet groans of the dying:
   then, Lord, that cry from the pits of hell, a cry
      to the forsaking God.

Lord, since that moment, all nature has been replying:
   the sky, sullen and ashen, has rent itself like a mourner,
      tearing the garment of cloud with lightning, and
      protesting in the speech of thunder;
   the earth has rocked, men cling to one another, soldiers
      unflinching in battle look from one to the other
      in fear;
      they say, Lord, that the tombs of the prophets

have erupted, and in the Temple the wall before
the Holy Place has been torn from top to bottom;
and Lord, this darkness—has the sun hid for shame?
Is it the shadow of God over us, or nature
covering our deeds lest they destroy us?
Lord, is this the end? The end of us?
Our evil revealed in what we have done to You,
are we now damned?
Lord, give us peace, end this tempest, command
these elements as You did in Galilee.

You have spoken the word, Lord, the word of Him returning
as a warrior out of the tumult of holy war,
I hear that word, flung defiantly into darkness and
chaos:

IT IS FINISHED!

I hear that word, Lord, and waiting prophets hear it;
dreamers and visionaries, those whose search was
for truth and whose passion was for justice,
Gabriel, Michael, angel and archangel, the Messengers
of Bethlehem,
humankind, remembering our father Adam before he hid
from God;
creation with the remembrance and promise of Eden's
Garden
—with joy they hear, It is finished.

This day is the prophets' word incarnate, sacrificial truth.
This day the Bethlehem child has run His course and finished
the work that was given Him to do.
This day, God is revealed to men, and Adam's enmity
is reconciled:

This day, creation is in travail, the birth-pangs
 of the cross are upon it, the new heaven
 and new earth are assured.

You hear that word too, you satanic powers,
  estranging us from God,
  holding us ransom in guilt and fear,
  darkening life with taunts of an eternity yours
   neither to give nor destroy, and clouding
   death with uncertainty,
  desiring us that you might sift us like chaff
   —you hear it, for these words are written on
  your grave.
   They are your last rites, your committal, death
   to death, hades to hades.

Lord Jesus Christ, it is finished!
 The day on Calvary cannot be revoked.
 The day on Calvary is the Last Day,
  the End is written:
  we are redeemed and we wait the
   final consummation of all things.

A Prayer for Others:
  for all who win the only victories that
   matter any more,
   love over hatred,
   truth over falsehood,
   hope over despair.

82

FAITH

The Word: Luke 23 v. 46

Jesus said, Father, into Thy hands I commend my spirit.

LORD, it is dying that threatens us, not death:
      our fear of pain,
      the procession of a life-time's memories that pass
         before us in a moment,
      the final losing of what is familiar;
   this is the valley of the shadow of death.

Lord, in Your last journey upon this cross, You have redeemed
   us,
      this journey of unspeakable pain,
      borne with the memories of Nazareth, Galilee and
      Bethany,
      in this place so starkly hostile;
      and now, Lord, You drink the last of the draught,
      the death of Man, the last heart-beat, the loss
      of pain in oblivion.
      This is death, and here there is no terror;
      in faith
      and obedience You came to this cross,

endured all its pain, and now in faith
You die.

You are laying down Your life, Lord, trusting in Him Who is
    able to
raise the dead to life,
        to bring victory out of defeat,
            incorruption out of corruption,
            honour out of dishonour,
            immortality out of mortality,
            life out of death,
    the God of Abraham, Isaac, and Jacob,
    the God of the living and the
    dead, the God who raises the fallen.

You are dying, Lord, believing that Resurrection is the last
    word and not death,
    that You will again break bread in the upper room
    with Your disciples, with the eleven,
    and with the countless millions who
    shall be their heirs in
    all generations;
    that You will walk again with the disillusioned and
    perplexed, and
    Your words will be like fire banishing the
    chill of unbelief;
    that the church, to be brought to birth by
    Your Spirit at Pentecost,
    will celebrate cross and resurrection,
    the death and the unending life,
    knowing the joy of Your presence
    among men.

Lord Jesus, our dying and our death are yet to come, and
     how they shall
  come, or when, we know not;
  we may pray now that we may not be afraid, but
  our faith
     is not always strong enough to say
     that we shall not be,
  we hope we may have courage to bear whatever may be
  the ills of our
     last journey, but we know our own
     cowardice;
     our humanity shrinks from pain and
     sudden shock.
This life we know, but the next . . .? Our
cracked city pavements
     are more sure signs of reality
     to us than streets paved
     with gold.

Lord, You we know, and in You the Father;
  teach us, Lord, that this is enough, for this
  is life—
     to know the one true God,
     and Jesus Christ Whom He has sent;
     may we, day by day, commend our spirits into
     Your hands,
          commend our work and responsibilities,
          our homes and families,
          our loves so precious and so vulnerable,
          our dreams and our hopes,
          our life among men,
          our responsibility to our neighbour here

and beyond our sight across
the world:
that when our last day comes, we may know
those hands into
which death delivers us, as the
hands that have carried us
throughout our lives.

Lord, into Your hands we commend our spirits . . .
for He Who raised Our Lord Jesus from the dead,
shall raise us up also, and freely with Him, give
us all things.
Brethren, the Lord is risen!
He is risen indeed!

A Prayer for Others:

remember those who are dying,
those who have lived without faith,
that they may die with faith,
those who have lived in the faith of
Christ, that they may see the
celestial city.

V

He is Here,
He is Now

The Prayers in this Section are based on
The Resurrection of Christ

1

THE GARDEN

The Word: John 20 vv. 1–18

LORD, we find grief hard to bear,
    sometimes the weight of it grows lighter
        —time heals, they say, but there is a grief for
        which eternity would be too short—
    it belongs not to our present, but to our past,
        without pity it pulls us back along
        the way of memory, habit, familiar things,
        and reminds us of
            what once we had,
            what used to be,
            what is no longer.
And so, Lord, we are driven back to time past,
    to the tomb that houses the dead,
    that was to us warmth, life, kindness, love, companionship,
        to keep vigil with our memories,
        unbearable, because they are filled with
            what no longer exists,
        inescapable, because without this burden
            we have nothing.

There are tears, Lord,

people say we shouldn't shed them, they expect us to
be composed and brave, to disguise our feelings and keep
them private; tears, they say, are only
upsetting to other people,
    —but You have given us tears, Lord,
        a sacrament of our bodies,
        an outward and visible sign of an
        inner and spiritual truth,
        an expression of the inexpressible,
        saying what our lips cannot say;
    tears are the physical, tangible signs that our
    grief is to do with flesh and blood, with the
    things our eyes have seen, our ears have heard,
    our hands have touched.

She came that morning, Lord,
    to sit by the tomb, alone with grief,
    Mary, whom You forgave, made whole,
        raised, blessed;
    she came because it seemed that grief could do
    only futile things, watch and remember;
    soon there would be the last act of love, the
    anointing, disguising the stench of death with fragrance,
    and, after that, watch and remember;
    and through eyes, blinded with tears,
        the present had no reality,
        the garden could have been a desert,
        parched and pitiless, it would have made no
            difference,
        the gardener could have been anyone,
            anyone at all.

Until out of the present

there came the word that filled
    that moment with grace
    and the future with hope.
Lord, it was such a simple word,
    not a sound of trumpets,
    not a profound word,
        ponderous with learning,
        brilliant with insight,
    it was such a simple word, Lord,
    —You called her name.

A Prayer for Others:

    that the resurrection faith may be given to
        those in the hour of their greatest need,
        the sad, the bereaved, the dying.

2

THE FIRST EVENING

The Word: John 20 vv. 19–20

LORD, fear locks us in,
    it bolts and bars the door,
    it cuts us off from the world around us,
    it reduces the dimension of our lives,
        like four walls crushing in upon us,
        rendering us powerless, futile, isolated.

It is fear of what lies the other side of our locked doors
    that keeps us shivering in our hide-outs, Lord,
    for we think we know too well what the world does
    to people who believe as we do:
        it betrays them,
        it is unjust to them,
        it is cruel,
        it has the power to crucify them;
        so the fear that there are powers
        beyond our locked doors that can
        destroy us, keeps us inside,
        preserving our lives, such as they are,
        the living death of the shuttered room.

Lord, we are persuaded that nothing can happen

beyond those doors that will make any difference;
    let us stay here and talk to one another,
        they won't understand us outside;
        let us reminisce together and be grateful we
        have our memories, the people outside do
        not share them;
        let us remain here until the world forgets us,
        and we can unlock the doors and go out
        unrecognized;
        let us stay where we are secure, because
        everything outside is damned.

Lord, how often is it so,
    the church locked in behind its open doors,
    trapped in the traditions we are afraid to
        change,
    talking to one another a language that we
        believe others cannot understand, a language
        meant to communicate Good News to every
        son of man,
    discussing evangelism, because this will leave
        us no time to evangelise,
    afraid of putting anything at risk, because we have
        seen what the world does,
    saving our lives, and losing them.

Lord, Risen Jesus,
    beyond those doors the tomb is empty,
    out there You have triumphed.
    The world stands beneath Your Lordship;
        come to us, before fear makes an
            end of us,
        come, through all the barriers we
            have erected,

come, and may Your word of peace cast out
the seven devils of fear.

A Prayer for Others:
    for Christians who are frightened by change,
      who see God clearly in yesterday,
      dimly in today,
      and never in tomorrow,
    for men who are paralysed by fear in any guise,
      that Christ may heal them.

3

THOMAS

The Word: John 20 vv. 24–29

LORD, he listened to them,
    their excited voices almost incoherent as they stammered
        out what had happened,
    their eyes bright with certainty, too bright
        for their word to be trusted;
            men believing what they wanted
                to believe?
            unbearable grief breaking into
                insane delusion?

For him, there was only the evidence of his own eyes,
    the man of freedom led trussed
        from a garden,
    the man of justice unfairly
        tried and condemned,
    the man of gentleness dragged as a
        criminal to the place of execution,
    the man of love tortured on
        a cross,
    the man of faith lowered dead from
        the gibbet, wrapped in a shroud,

the man of hope sealed in the
    cold grave;
—this was the evidence of his own eyes,
    events that had come as sudden as a
    Galilean storm, at first unbelievable, contrary
    to all they trusted and hoped for,
    the reign of love, the kingship of
    Messiah, but now believed—
        the evidence was overwhelming;
        Jesus lay dead in the tomb,
        and only the evidence of eye,
        hand and ear could expunge the
        black stain from the memories that
        filled his heart.

Lord, we have the evidence of our eyes,
    we have seen and heard of injustice, oppression,
    ruthlessness:
        men and women tread out their days in
        the prisons of Spain, Greece, Russia, China,
        without trial or redress, convicted of no crime
        save their claim to freedom of speech, thought,
        belief and worship;
        the world still favours the rich and deprives
        the poor,
        applauds might and ridicules gentleness;
        the widow and the aged count out their
        pennies in a society fat-bellied in
        its affluence.

Yet, Lord, it is in such a world that we encounter You,
    the evidence of Christ risen given to those
    blessed who have not seen, yet believe,

for in the torn flesh of humanity we
see Your pierced hands, and
in our broken communities the
wounded side,
      Your presence lets loose in the world compassion
      and truth, so because You are risen the cry
      is not unheard, the falsehood cannot prevail,
      the unjust are weighed in the balance, the
      powerful crushed by their own power.

Lord, You are on every side,
    I cannot escape You,
    and the sight of You draws from me the only
      words sufficient for what I have seen and touched—
      My Lord and my God!

A Prayer for Others:
    remember those who, by temperament or training,
      find doubt more natural than faith,
    and those who, faced with evidence,
      are also faced with decision.

4

EMMAUS

The Word: Luke 24 vv. 13–35

LORD, the last time they trod this road
    they were going the opposite way,
    walking with quick, confident step,
    for time was short, the waiting days were
        nearly at an end,
        the promise of prophets was about to be
            fulfilled,
        the prayers of Israel's sons, soaked in
        generations of suffering, were about to be
            answered,
        the tyranny of Rome, and every remembered
        tyranny with which Israel had borne, was
        about to be broken,
            from out of Israel, Messiah had risen,
                mighty in word and deed,
                Jesus of Nazareth.

That was last week, Lord,
    and this is the same road,
    but they will not be quick to dream again,
    and in days to come faith will be difficult,
        and hope almost impossible,

for the world has not changed,
Messiah has not come,
>or, if he has, in terror we have seen him defeated,
>and the world remains in Satan's grip.

Lord, I know that road;
>there have been enterprises begun with
>enthusiasm that came to nothing,
>times when I believed that dreams were
>best kept to oneself rather than
>put at risk in a hostile world,
>there has been disappointment, and the
>hurt that is worst of all, of
>looking for a salvation that didn't
>come;
>if Emmaus road is lonely, then we must grieve
>not only for our dreams, but also for mankind
>unvisited and unredeemed.

Lord, there is a Presence;
>we see it in the Word, the pages turn, the Law and
>the prophets, the words we have known since our
>youth are repeated, the promises are heard;
>and as words and promises leap up to our
>eyes, what was familiar and known by heart is
>unknown and strange and compelling and full of
>truth; we had seen but had not comprehended, we
>had heard but had not listened, but now, the words
>pour into our minds and hearts, and in the fire
>of the present and the Presence become
>>the Word,
>>Christ,
>>Risen,
>>>for so the scriptures said it would be.

Lord, there is a Presence,
>You come in to remain with us,
>and in an action that stirs up the memory
>we recognize You;
>again and again,
>You are made known to us
>>in the breaking of bread.

A Prayer for Others:
>*those for whom things haven't worked out*
>*in the way that they had hoped,*
>*that life may bless them in ways*
>*they had never dreamed.*

THE SHORE

The Word: John 21 vv. 1–14

LORD, it was a familiar world they returned to that night,
    the world of their work
    and that of their fathers before them;
  it was a part of them,
    the sound of grinding sand and shingle
      as they pushed the boat from the
      shore,
    the lap of the waters on the prow
      as it cut its way across
      Galilee,
    the sting of spray on the cold night
      air,
    the twine of the nets cutting into their
      hands as they hauled them about for
      a catch,
    the night hours filled with work.

Lord, the world of our work is just as familiar,
    the clatter of typewriters, rustling papers,
    carbons, telephones ringing their unmusical
    bells;

the savage shriek of wood-saws, the hum
of electric motors, the smell of sawdust,
the feel of wood-grain;
cold metal, fashioned with precision, bathed
in oil, gas fumes filling the lungs, the
rhythmic power of internal combustion;
ink, stiff ledgers, clinking coins,
comptometers with staccato action like
soldiers on parade;
slot-machine coffee, cafeteria meals, jolting
buses and over-crowded trains,
this is our world, Lord.

And sometimes, Lord, we grow weary of it;
the work we do every day seems futile, there
is no end-product, it does no good for anyone,
hours of toil seem only to leave us empty-handed,
and the pay-envelope is little compensation for
the feeling that we have achieved nothing;
so it seems, Lord, until we see You there,
giving meaning and direction to what we do,
showing us the wealth in what we thought were
empty waters.

Lord, You came that morning,
had breakfast with Your disciples,
called them to be apostles,
and for the second time they left their
nets, to go out and bear witness to the resurrection;
there are not many of us that You call
away from our jobs, Lord; most of us
have to stay there and work out our
apostolate among familiar things;

and it is there that You come
to us,
at every dawn You call us,
and breakfast is communion.

A Prayer for Others:
    remember those whose daily work has been
        a service to you today,
    pray for people with monotonous and
        unrewarding jobs,
    and for Christians who are tempted to separate
        Sunday from Monday.

6

THE ASCENSION

The Word: Acts 1 vv. 1–12

LORD, we do not often stand on the holy mountain,
    where the vision rivets our eyes and makes us
        reluctant to look away to the grey
        world around us;
    the swirling clouds, the Christ in glory,
        the light that penetrates us; the
        glimpse of life that is more than our
        present life, making us impatient for
        the reality behind the shadows; the
        paradise that now we see and now we do
        not see, that now is ours and still
        is not yet ours; and Jesus who is with
        us, yet taken from our sight:
    Lord, these signs are not for analysis, the holy mountain
        is not a place to stand and discuss the merits of
        what we have seen, nor analyse the state of our souls
        or the prospects for the Kingdom;
        it is the place of affirmation and ringing doxology,
        to which all prayer has ascended, pouring all faith,
        and hope, and love into the crucible of glory where
        the last things are forged and shaped, and history's

last chapter written as the prayer,
"Thine is the Kingdom,
the Power,
and the Glory,
forever and ever":
Lord, on the holy mountain we do not
speculate, we worship.

Such moments are not often given to us, Lord;
our worship becomes limited by habit,
we gather at our appointed times and in suitable
places, as You have commanded us, and we offer
our acts of worship;
we know that what we do in Your house is meant
to deepen our sense of Your glory, yet so often
it serves to insulate us against it,
to protect us from holiness
to guard us against awe;
our four walls contain us and overshadow us,
and sometimes we try to make them contain You, and
overshadow You.

Lord, in this day bring us again to the holy mountain,
that we may see Christ, transcendent, filling
earth and sky with glory,
that our worship may be liberated
and wonder strip away our sophistication;
may we gaze at our glimpses of glory,
and know in our hearts
ascending love,
adoration,
joy,
assurance,
and faith.

A Prayer for Others:

> *for the church at its worship*
>> *that it may not judge the triumph of the Christian*
>> *faith in terms of numbers*
>> *but in the power of the risen Christ to create*
>> *faith, hope and love in human hearts.*

7

PENTECOST

The Word: Acts 2 vv. 1–4

LORD, we want another Pentecost, a revival of the Spirit's
    power among us,
      so we look back with nostalgia to the first
    Pentecost, envying the apostles that experience
    that seems to elude us;
      for we want to hear the wind in the streets,
      rattling the windows and banging the doors, blowing
      gusty and invigorating from the mountain of the Lord,
      we want to see the tongues of fire over each
    other's heads,
      we want to preach the word that converts, renews,
    convicts, redeems,
              Lord, we want another Pentecost . . .

At least, Lord, that's what we ask for,
    I'm not sure whether we really *want* it;
    I ask myself, Lord, do I know what I am praying for?
        —the wind, Lord, the wind,
        blowing open doors I thought were safely shut;
        hurling neat plans, agendas, committee reports
        into the air;
        rushing down by-ways where men have been snoring

peacefully in the siesta of middle-age;
—and the fire, Lord,
that flame that is not a cosy glow,
keeping me pink and warm, but a flame that
sears, scalds, consumes (remember Malachi, Lord:
refining fire and fuller's soap, the men nearest
to God purged and scrubbed);
that flame that makes me shield my eyes, and
sweat.

Lord, this is what I am asking for,
may I also *want* it:
and if You come, Lord, still as wind and fire, yet
unannounced and unseen by others, may I recognize You;
as I look for the renewal of Your church, Lord, may I
be prepared for the renewal within myself: the wind
that drives out the dust and debris of my half-hearted
efforts and my shabby compromises, that makes me
catch my breath and clutch again the security of the Rock;
and the fire, Lord, the passion for You and people which
might, by Your grace, forge something of lasting gold in
my life.

Lord, we want another Pentecost
that, renewed by wind and fire, we may
preach the Good News,
and men may hear,
and hearing, may see visions and dream dreams.

A Prayer for Others:
that the Church that prays for the coming of
the Holy Spirit
may be given grace to endure His coming
and may He be poured out on
all men.

108

VI

Hear Me, Lord

The Prayers in this Section are based on
The Encounter with Life

1

LONELINESS

The Word: Matthew 26 vv. 36–46

Could you not watch with me one hour?

Lord, the night is lonely,
  the darkness wraps us, each in his own world,
      and no night is more lonely, or darkness deeper,
      than Gethsemane's night:
      the others do not understand, their world is dark
          only because their eyes are closed in
          sleep.
  You tried to explain, Lord,
      as You knelt and washed their feet,
      speaking of service,
      as You broke bread, passed the
      crumbling pieces from hand to hand,
      speaking of a body broken,
      as You handed them a cup, speaking of
      a new covenant, sealed in Your blood;
  water, bread, wine, washing, body, blood, vine,
  Comforter, love, life, death, life
      —they blinked their bewilderment; in three days

      they shall begin to understand, but not yet;
      now, they have fallen asleep.
Lord, we are sometimes lonely because we cannot make our-
    selves understood;
      there is nothing more personal than fear,
      locked up inside us,
      a feeling without any rational explanation.
      Others may sleep peacefully in Gethsemane,
      but we see the trees in the moonlight, their contorted
        branches frozen in the mad dance of death:
      trees, how could the others understand what our fears
        have made of them?
      Loneliness robs us of language, and others of under-
        standing.

Look, Lord, at these lonely ones,
      a woman, basket in hand (enough food for one),
      returning from the shops where she has spoken to
      another human being for the first time since yesterday
      and for the last time until tomorrow, unlocks her
      door and reluctantly shuts it, nobody to be shut
      out, only herself to be shut in:
      a man, on hospital bed, the family visited
      yesterday evening, and now he awaits the theatre-
        trolley,
      to be carried into anaesthetized oblivion, and none
      can enter with him;
      a minister, remembering his call, the fire that
      burned in his belly and tempered his heart,
      going to meet a regiment of empty pews,
      to worship in a museum of Victorian nonconformity,
      to break bread with the dwindling few, looking
      for the resurrection. . . .

Lord, hear the prayer You uttered for them,
    watch with them this hour
    and the next.

A Prayer for Others:
    remember a lonely person, perhaps aged, bereaved, or
        because the family is away from home,
    pray for them,
    and then go and visit them.

2

DECREE ABSOLUTE

The Word: Ephesians 5 vv. 25–33

LORD, it is ten years since she came to meet the man she
    loved in Your house:
        that wedding day,
                day of gifts, relations half-known, friends,
                    gleaming
                limousines, urgent photographers, flowers, organ,
                confetti, bride's-maids, father:
                and she, sheathed in white dress, radiant with
                this day's beauty:
                a bride, receiving the pledge of love, signified
                in a ring, sealed in the blessing of the Holy Spirit,
                joined to her man in the most ancient of
                    covenants.

They were happy, Lord,
                with love full of the promise that the years
                would drive deeper roots into their lives, until mind,
                heart and understanding were one, as
                the flesh was one.
                You gave them two sons, Lord, and they gave
                them apostolic names—missionary and martyr—for

they too were full of promise for the
years to come.

They were happy, Lord,
> and she loved him
> > —what lust entered his eyes that he should
> > look at another woman?
> > what vandalism ordered his actions that he
> > with one desire should take another from
> > her husband, leave his own wife bereft,
> > and his sons fatherless?
> > what confusion seized his mind that he
> > should judge her to have fallen short of all
> > that he required, in things other than love,
> > fidelity, caring, sympathy, motherhood?

Lord, now she is alone with her sons,
> sustained by a faith in Christ, made stronger by
> what she has experienced.
> They speak of her courage, Lord, and the laughter that
> > still brings alive the beauty of that face he
> > once loved; they speak of her ability in being
> > mother and father to her two sons; they say, Lord,
> > she is better off without him.
> But, Lord, You see it, don't You?
> The sadness that in a moment passes across her features,
> > giving to her face years that do not yet belong to her:
> The anxiety she feels for her responsibility—how can she
> > compensate for what her children have lost, how
> > to be a father to them, as well as mother?
> And it is her nature to love. Her bed is lonely, and
> > only she knows the desolation of one who once was
> > caressed, kissed, held, entered, in the ecstasy of
> > bodily union.

Lord, in another month the divorce decree will be declared
    absolute—
        absolute, the sundering of the bond:
        absolute, the breaking of the Covenant:
        absolute, the undoing of all that was done in
        Your house ten years ago:
        absolute, love's betrayal.

Lord, she has to build again, knowing now that the work of
    our hands, and our most committed ideals, can be
    wantonly destroyed:
    she has to live for today and tomorrow, bearing
    the burden of yesterday's memories:
    she has to endeavour to succeed, though she never
    be sure whether it was she who failed.

Lord, may she know that it is not only the breaking of
    the covenant that is absolute:
    Your faithfulness is absolute:
    she has put her trust in You, Lord: may
    what has been salvaged from yesterday be
    the sure foundation of tomorrow.

A Prayer for Others:
    for those whose marriage is threatened by
        failure, incompatibility, infidelity or circumstance,
    for husbands and wives facing each other across
        a divorce court,
    for the children of broken marriages.

3

FELLOWSHIP

The Word: Philippians 2 vv. 1–11

LORD, loneliness is poverty, it is a deprivation,
    fellowship is wealth.
How casually I hold my wealth,
    taking for granted the people who are part of my
    life simply because they are familiar.
They are everywhere:
the lad in the newsstand, as cheerful as the comics,
insists on calling me "Sir";
the people at work, Stan always on about the government,
Johnny, who is always going to win the bet next week,
the boss, dynamic and dyspeptic,
Melanie, the office-girl, discussing her latest date
(we've never met him, but she assures us he looks
just like Pat Boone);
the ticket-collecter, sad-eyed from watching the trains go by;
the folk at the church, nothing else in the world could
bring such a mixed bunch together, straight out of
"Pilgrim's Progress"—Faithful, Valiant-for-Truth,
    Doubtful, Worldly Wiseman, Hopeful,
and some still looking for the wicket gate;
the family, and all the signs that they are alive and well,

coats hanging in the closet, Action Man on the stairs, the
latest artistic masterpiece "My Friend" on a bedroom wall,
food in the cupboard that I didn't put there,
flowers that I didn't arrange:
Lord, they are alive and well, thank You.

Lord, You have given us all to each other,
each of us weaves his life like a tapestry, with a
multitude of threads, the threads of affection, service,
dependence,
so that others are woven into our tapestry and are
part of it,
and, Lord, this is my fear,
for love has woven so many into my life, and I
have already known what it is for some to be
wrenched away,
to gaze in dismay when one was torn from the tapestry,
leaving torn edges, broken threads, raw heart,
numbed mind, the deeper the love, the greater the loss.

Lord, You have come into the pattern of our lives,
Your Presence is there in the midst of every relationship
("Where two or three are gathered . . ."),
and You give permanency to our love, hope to our faith;
our lives are held in You, You have woven eternal life
into our all too transitory existence.

A Prayer for Others:

*Remember the human relationships that
God has given us.
Remember how much we have taken for
granted in our day.
Remember those who fill out the pattern
of our lives.*

4

COMMUNION

The Word: John 15 vv. 12–17

LORD, the way that led to man's communion with God was
    long,
        dark and flinty,
but it was not we who trod it;
the milestones of sacrifice marked it,
        the surrender of wealth for poverty, the
        kingdom, the power and the glory for bondage,
        weakness and anonymity;

        the pangs of death endured for the healing
        that might come from the breaking of one
        man's body,
        the offering of life, set free from fear,
        joyous and compassionate:

        but ours was not the wealth surrendered,
        it was not we who died,
        our life was not the offering made.

Lord, we did not come to quell the anger in Your heart,
    nor make a gift to appease Your wrath, we did not

gather all our human resources to make terms of peace,
under-written with our most valued possessions,
we did not reconcile You, compelling You by our
    persistent faith
to turn Your face to us again,
we did not heal the wounds in Your heart, nor span the
    gulf
between God and man,

> we did not quit heaven for earth,
> we did not stand trial,
> it was not us whom they crucified. . . .

Lord, it was Christ who came to us,

> You gave His wealth to us in our poverty,
> You bore the anger of our hearts, the insults of our lips,
> You reconciled us, healed our wounds, died our deaths,
> You turned our sulking faces,
> You led us joyously into life;

> > and Christ was the gift
> > and His blood the price
> > and His resurrection the assurance
> > and all of it was grace.

Lord, this I believe,
> and insofar as I believe, it is grace,
> by this faith I live,
> and insofar as I am faithful, it is grace.
> I offer whatever is mine to offer
> > and every gift I make is the gift of
> > Your grace.

A Prayer for Others:

> *Let us pray for those whose*
> *healing is not yet begun,*
> *the hostile, the indifferent,*
> *the unforgiven and the unforgiving,*
> *who have yet to know the*
> > *Resurrection.*

5

HEAR ME, LORD

The Word: Psalm 139 vv. 1–18

LORD, I believe You listen,
  and for You there is eternity to spare,
    time to hear our words,
    and, more important, the voice
        of mind and heart that cannot
        find words,
    time to listen to what we are saying,
        though all men cry to You,
        and the world has need of You,
        and nations rise,
        and sparrows fall,
        yet still, it is as if You
        had no one else to listen to.

So I dare to carry in my thoughts the
  needs of the thousands and of the one;
    I do not listen enough,
    I hear their words, but not
        what they are saying,
    I accept the obvious meaning,
        and ignore the real meaning,

the hesitant sentence that is
a cry for help,
the joviality that keeps
loneliness at bay,
the busy chatter that locks
out conversation;
yet I bring them to You,
their words,
what I have heard and failed
to hear,
knowing that You will listen and
You will understand.

I dare to come,
I dare not stay away:
other people, Lord—I carry them, and am
carried,
but the weight is sometimes too much,
I shut my ears to the burden of
their words,
and the world that would break my back
—but not in prayer:
in prayer, You listen, and
You hear the words I have heard,
and You take the weight that
is too much for my frailty,
and Your compassion bears them,
as it bears me.
That is why I come to You, Lord,
for prayer is Your listening more than
my speaking:
my request is also my trust,
Hear me, Lord.

MY PRAYER PROJECTS